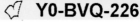

Y0-BVQ-226

My Little Book of Special Prayers

Written and compiled by
Felicity Henderson

Illustrations by
Toni Goffe

A LION BOOK

Tring . Batavia . Sydney

Special days

Thank you, God,
for special days to look forward to,
and special days to remember.

Sunday

Dear God,
Sunday is your special day.
We go to church,
we sing songs
and we learn about Jesus.
I like Sundays!

Christmas

It's nearly Christmas,
when it's Jesus' birthday.
Thank you, God, for baby Jesus.

Easter

Good Friday is a time of sadness,
Easter is a time of gladness.
On Good Friday Jesus died,
But rose again at Eastertide.
All thanks and praise to God.

Birthdays

Birthdays are special days.
Thank you, God,
for birthdays and balloons,
and parties and presents.
It's my birthday today!
Thank you for this special day.

At Grandma's house

When I stay at Grandma's house,
everything's different.
But if Grandma's there,
everything's all right,
because she looks after me.
Please, God, look after me
and Grandma.

A day out

Thank you, God, for a lovely day out.
Thank you for the trip,
and all the different things we saw.
It's been a great day!

The new baby

Dear God, it's a very special day.
We've got a new baby in our family.
Thank you, God,
that you love my new baby
and that you love me, too.

Vacations

Thank you, God, for my vacation.
Thank you for making
the sea and the sand.
And thank you for buckets and
sand-shovels and ice-creams.
Dear God, thank you for the seashore.

I'm not feeling very well

Dear God, I'm not feeling very well.
Thank you for the people who look after
me, and help me to get better soon.

My friend's coming to stay

Dear God, I'm so excited.
My friend is coming to stay

the night at our house.
We can have lots of fun.
Thank you for my friend.

Mom's birthday

Today it's my mom's birthday.
I made a special present
to give to her.
She's the best mom in the world!
Thank you, God, for my mom.

God bless us!

May the Lord bless us and take care of us;
may the Lord be kind and gracious to us;
may the Lord look down on us with favor
and give us peace.

Copyright © 1988 Lion Publishing
Illustrations copyright © 1988 Toni Goffe

Published by
Lion Publishing plc
Icknield Way, Tring, Herts, England
ISBN 0 7459 1253 2
Lion Publishing Corporation
1705 Hubbard Avenue, Batavia, Illinois 60510, USA
ISBN 0 7459 1253 2
Albatross Books Pty Ltd
PO Box 320, Sutherland, NSW 2232, Australia
ISBN 0 86760 943 5

First edition 1988

Acknowledgments
Copyright prayers as follows:
'Good Friday is a time of sadness' from *Pray About,*
Church Information Office

Printed and bound in Singapore